W

M000189421

Advent and Christmas
2015–2016

Genevieve Glen
Jerome Kodell

LITURGICAL PRESS
Collegeville, Minnesota

www.litpress.org

Nihil Obstat: Reverend Robert Harren, *Censor deputatus.*
Imprimatur: ✛ Most Reverend Donald J. Kettler, J.C.L., Bishop of
Saint Cloud, Minnesota. March 6, 2015.

Cover design by Monica Bokinskie. Cover photo © Thinkstock.

ISSN: 1550-803X
ISBN: 978-0-8146-4970-1   978-0-8146-4996-1 (ebook)

Introduction

Welcome to rehearsal! Every liturgical season is a rehearsal for the seasons of life, which follow a calendar of their own.

Advent and Christmas offer us exercise in the art of "waiting in joyful hope." It sounds simple enough, but of course it isn't. Waiting has many moods: impatience, expectation, dread, eagerness, reluctance, confidence, and anxiety. And that's probably a partial list.

Waiting is one of life's inevitabilities, but joyful hope is not. Joy is not false gaiety waiting with gritted teeth. It is a fruit of our communion with Christ in the Spirit of God, but it must sometimes be snatched back from the grip of self-pity. Hope is not wishful thinking leapfrogging over the present into a rosy future. It is a gift given to us at baptism, but it must sometimes be retrieved from the jaws of despair. The qualities God gives us are always ours to use, but they are apt to remain pale little shoots of possibility unless we strengthen them by practice, practice, practice.

What scripts and role models do Advent and Christmas offer us for our practice sessions? Before Christmas, Advent proffers the long history of God's people waiting down millennia for the savior first promised in the Garden of Eden. But it also hints that the wait will not be over by Christmas. Although the promise has been kept with the birth of Christ, it will not be brought to completion until he returns in glory to close the play with the final entry of God's eternal reign.

Christmas offers encouragement and warning as we study the parts played by those who welcomed Christ—Mary and

Joseph, shepherds and magi, Simeon and Anna, disciples and saints, the hungry, the lepers, the blind, the sick—and those who rejected him—King Herod, those who stoned St. Stephen, even the unconverted Saul of Tarsus.

But the figure who best embodies waiting in joyful hope during Advent and Christmas is Mary, the Mother of Jesus. Before her Son is born, she teaches us the art of expectancy. Despite all potential hindrances, including near rejection by her betrothed, her song is the *Magnificat* as she prepares her child for birth and her world to receive him. That's right: expectancy is not just sitting around till something happens; it is actively welcoming what is to come and making everything ready for it.

After her Son is born, Mary protects and nurtures him toward the day when he will leave her to take up his mission, a day hinted at repeatedly in the Christmas season liturgies. Mary is rarely seen after Christmas week, but she is surely always there in the background, making everything ready, as we must, for the coming reign of God.

So, take up the playbook. The rehearsals are about to begin!

FIRST WEEK OF ADVENT

A Wake-Up Call

Readings: Jer 33:14-16; 1 Thess 3:12–4:2; Luke 21:25-28, 34-36

Scripture:
May the Lord make you increase and abound in love
   for one another and for all,
   just as we have for you,
   so as to strengthen your hearts,
   to be blameless in holiness before our God and Father
   at the coming of our Lord Jesus with all his holy ones.
      (1 Thess 3:12-13)

Reflection: My five-year-old nephew had been excited for days because grandmother was coming to visit. He was up early on the day itself and at his parents' bedside. "Is she here yet?" "No, she'll be here after lunch." "Oh."

By breakfast he had a solution: "Let's eat lunch early!"

The season of Advent is a time of expectation. The Lord is coming! Wake up! Get ready! We probably cannot hope to be aroused to my nephew's fever pitch, but the church puts us in touch with the eagerness of the early Christians at Thessalonica: "[S]trengthen your hearts"! "[B]e blameless in holiness"!

The Thessalonians who first read Paul's letter were only a few years removed from Jesus' ascension and were expecting him to return in glory any day. The church had to deal with some extremes: Why work if the end is near? With the passage of years the church realized that it might be a long time before Jesus came a second time. That brought other problems. The delay could make us forget or become complacent about his coming.

That is where we are today. The First Sunday of Advent comes as a surprise in the humdrum of our daily lives. We are running around as usual, from one task to the next, one busy day to the next, when suddenly here it is again. What? Is it that time of the year again?

The church encourages us to slow down, to refocus, to wait for the coming of the Lord in quiet hope. The idea of the Lord's coming has expanded since the time of the Thessalonians. We still look forward to his coming in glory at the end of time, but we concentrate more now on preparing ourselves for his present coming in grace and we look back to his first coming, the incarnation, to understand what it means for us.

Meditation: Did the season of Advent catch you by surprise? How do you feel about the coming of the Lord into your life during these days? What will you do to prepare?

Prayer: Lord Jesus, you know where we are on our spiritual journey. We want to meet you in a new way during these days, so that we may recognize your face in the people we might otherwise overlook or avoid.

The Go-Between

Readings: Rom 10:9-18; Matt 4:18-22

Scripture:
[H]e saw two brothers,
  Simon who is called Peter, and his brother Andrew.
    (Matt 4:18)

Reflection: When I read Andrew's story, I remember Donald. He was an ordinary kid, a C-something student in my first junior high English class, someone you wouldn't usually notice. But he would notice you.

One hot, sticky afternoon, in a room steaming with adolescent energy, I discovered that I had mislaid my keys for at least the fortieth time. Right before my frustration erupted into misfortune for my hapless students, I caught sight of the truant keys on the corner of my desk and Donald slipping quietly back into his seat. I suddenly realized it had happened before, more than once. Why I needed my keys so often, I don't remember now, but need them I did and lose them I did often. Whenever they disappeared, I had only to look up at Donald, and he would point me to them with his eyes, or he'd go and get them. He didn't do it for attention or thanks. Donald was an unusual boy, complete in himself, not needing others' approval, but always happy to serve.

Andrew was like that. He was one of the first four disciples Jesus called, but after that momentous day, he let Peter,

James, and John take the limelight while he slipped back into the shadows. He is often called "the brother of Peter," but Peter is never identified as "the brother of Andrew." But when anyone needed something, Andrew was there. In St. John's version of the story, John the Baptist directed him to Jesus, but instead of going after Jesus immediately, he went and brought his brother. When Jesus started looking for food to feed a hungry crowd, Andrew already knew that there was a boy with five barley loaves and two fish. When some Greeks asked Philip to take them to Jesus, Philip went and got Andrew first, and together they went to Jesus about it.

Among the disciples, Andrew was the go-to and the go-between, but he was never a get-between. He would have liked Donald.

Meditation: Who are the go-tos and the go-betweens in your world? Who are the get-betweens? Which one are you?

Prayer: Lord Jesus, you have called us all to be disciples. In your mercy, grant us the humility of St. Andrew, so that we may choose to live in your light rather than the limelight. Show us how to bring others to you and to make available whatever you want to use for their good.

December 1: Tuesday of the First Week of Advent

God or the Works of God

Readings: Isa 11:1-10; Luke 10:21-24

Scripture:
Blessed are the eyes that see what you see.
For I say to you,
    many prophets and kings desired to see what you see,
    but did not see it,
    and to hear what you hear, but did not hear it.
    (Luke 10:23-24)

Reflection: Six days after he was named coadjutor arch-bishop of Saigon, Fr. Francis Xavier Nguyen Van Thuan was imprisoned by the Communist government of Vietnam. He spent thirteen years from 1975 to 1988 in a "re-education camp," including nine in a solitary confinement without windows, in extreme heat and humidity. Lights would be left on for days and then turned off for days, leaving him in total darkness. He later commented that as terrible as this suffering was, his main torment came from his inability to minister to the desperate people in his diocese.

A turning point in his life came when he heard a voice saying to him, "Why do you torment yourself like this? You must distinguish between God and the works of God. Every-thing you have done and desire to continue doing [for your people] . . . are God's works, but *they* are not God! If God wants you to leave all of these works, do it right away and have faith in him!"

"To choose God and not the works of God," he later said. "This is the foundation of the Christian life in every age."

Jesus speaks in this same vein in today's gospel, making it all about personal relationship and knowledge of the Father, his own directly and that of his disciples through him. This is the great gift: "Blessed are the eyes that see what you see. / For I say to you, / many prophets and kings desired to see what you see, / but did not see it, / and to hear what you hear, but did not hear it."

Many disciples throughout history have made the sad mistake of overinvesting energy in the works of God, good works certainly, at the expense of a personal relationship with God and his Savior Son. The words of God to Archbishop Van Thuan are timely for busy disciples: "If God wants you to leave all of these works, do it right away and have faith in him!"

Meditation: Serving God is a beautiful calling. There are so many opportunities in spreading his word and ministering to many needs. How do you remain focused on God and not get distracted by his works?

Prayer: O God, you entrust many responsibilities to those who wish to serve you. Help us to serve you devotedly but never forget to make you, and not the works we do for you, the focus of our life.

December 2: Wednesday of the First Week of Advent

Hungry

Readings: Isa 25:6-10a; Matt 15:29-37

Scripture:
I do not want to send them away hungry. (Matt 15:32)

Reflection: Advent is a hungry season. Readings and prayers groan with longing for the Redeemer to come and find us, feed us, mend us, save us. But we're clever about disguising real hunger with little hunger pangs. The stores are already singing Christmas carols, and ads everywhere are trying to tell us what we're really hungry for: that special perfume, the latest e-toy, a bigger car.

Jesus knows real hunger, the hunger that claws at us beneath the skin of all that tinsel. When the crowds schlepped up the mountain to him, he knew they hadn't come for a sermon. They had brought their hungers with them—the lame, the blind, the deformed, the mute, and the people who loved and carried or led them. So he set about curing them at once.

And he knew that wasn't enough. The cures had taken awhile. Whatever food they had brought had run out. Jesus knew they needed bread, so he gave them bread, after he had taken it up and given thanks and broken it for them.

And he knew that wouldn't be enough, even with seven baskets of leftovers sitting there. He saw a couple of mothers looking anxiously at their kids: that was for today, but what will I feed them tomorrow? So he gave them a promise, written in sign language: look at those baskets of leftovers, take them home with you. There will be bread tomorrow.

It was only much later, and slowly, that his followers learned what he really meant by that. He said, "*I am the bread of life*" (John 6:35, emphasis added). He took the bread at the Last Supper table, gave thanks, broke it, and handed it around: "Take this, all of you, and eat of it, for this is my Body, which will be given up for you." And, so you won't ever run out, "Do this in memory of me."

Advent is a hungry season, but there are hungers hidden within hungers. Jesus knows what they are. Those items on your shopping list—what hungers will they feed? Your hunger to be thanked, or maybe just to get the shopping done? Or the recipients' hunger to be remembered, to be respected, to be known and understood, to be loved? "Do this in memory of me."

Meditation: Look at the names on your Christmas gift list. Spend some time thinking about each person. Try to imagine and list three real hungers that each one experiences. Is there a gift that might feed one of them?

Prayer: Lord Jesus, Bread of Life, we hunger for your presence, your word, your touch, your love. In your great mercy, grant us the grace to recognize our deepest hungers rather than to stop at feeding our superficial wants.

December 3:
Saint Francis Xavier, Priest (Catholic Church)
Thursday of the First Week of Advent (Episcopal Church)

The Eternal Rock

Readings: Isa 26:1-6; Matt 7:21, 24-27

Scripture:
Trust in the LORD forever!
    For the LORD is an eternal Rock. (Isa 26:4)

Reflection: In a memorable exchange in the movie *"Oh, God!"* supermarket manager Jerry Landers is speaking to his skeptical wife Bobbie about having seen and spoken with God. "I thought you believed in God," he says. "I do believe in God," she answers, "but I didn't know he really existed."

The faith of the prophet Isaiah is not so flimsy: "Trust in the LORD forever! / For the LORD is an eternal Rock." For Isaiah, God is not a disposable part of a misty cultural atmosphere but the center of the universe and the foundation of life, an eternal rock. There are many images for God in Scripture—shepherd, helmet, eagle, fortress—but the most frequent metaphor for God is rock. Like any metaphor, rock cannot be tied down to one interpretation. Some of the meanings are reliability, fidelity, and stability.

God as eternal rock is the basis for trust, and trust in God is the key to salvation. The New Testament word for this kind of trust is faith. "Go in peace; your faith has saved you."

Not go in peace because you can fully describe who I am or completely understand my purposes, but because you trust me as the way to eternal life. No human being merits this kind of trust, and many problems of believers today stem from misplacing faith/trust in human beings who are ministers and servants of God but not God.

An evident example is the havoc caused by the recent sexual abuse scandals in the church. People have left the church or even the Christian faith, by their own admission, because their faith in priests and bishops has been betrayed. If you can't trust them in this area, where can you trust them? This misses the point: We are not required to trust God's human representatives, but to trust God to do the work of salvation through weak and sinful ministers. The failure of God's representatives is not the failure of God.

Only God is an eternal Rock.

Meditation: Have you ever misplaced your trust and as a result been wounded? Are you trustworthy yourself?

Prayer: Lord, amid all the uncertainties of this world, help us to hold on to the one certainty, your faithfulness and love. Strengthen our trust in you so that we may be free from fear and be a rock for others.

Eyesight and Insight

Readings: Isa 29:17-24; Matt 9:27-31

Scripture:
Son of David, have pity on us! (Matt 9:27)

Reflection: It's getting darker earlier now, at least in the northern hemisphere. In this world of light switches and illumined clock faces, children may be the only ones who remember to be afraid of the dark. We all knew it once, the terror of human beings huddled in a cave at night, watching the gleaming eyes watching us from just beyond the dying fire. In the dark, we have little protection from predators either around or within us.

Perhaps the two blind men in the gospel story hung out together for the reassurance that they weren't alone in the dark in which they lived. Experience would have taught them to recognize the steps of frequent passersby. They obviously recognized Jesus. He lived in their town. They must have heard the town buzz about the wonders he had worked. So when he walked by, they got up and, with the uncanny skills of the blind, followed him to the house where he was staying.

They were clever beggars, though we don't know whether they begged for a living. They knew that if you keep your plea general enough, a hearer might give you more than you hoped for. All they asked for was pity. But Jesus saw straight through them. "Do you believe that I can do this?" he asked. He clearly didn't mean "toss you a few coins?" Yes, they said they believed he could. So he opened their eyes, with a curious rider, "Let it be done for you according to your faith."

What did he mean? He knew they did have faith. Like many of the blind, they couldn't see the surface of the world around them, but they could see something of the reality beneath its skin, as God does. Faith is "a share in God's seeing" (Adrienne von Speyr). With the eyes of faith, they had recognized him as the "Son of David," a messianic title many were not yet willing to use, and they asked him to do the impossible, restore their sight. Jesus confirmed their faith by granting their request, as if to match their eyes to their hearts, which could already see in the way that most mattered.

As the night closes in on us, whether outside or within, we might take a page from their playbook and call out, "Jesus, Son of David, have pity on us," seeking not bodily eyesight but faith's insight, lest we lose our way in the dark.

Meditation: What are your blind spots? What healing do you need?

Prayer: Jesus, Son of David, have pity on us, for we too are blind to our own failings and others' gifts. Open our eyes to see beneath the surface of our lives so that we may truly live by faith in you.

December 5: Saturday of the First Week of Advent

Foreground or Background

Readings: Isa 30:19-21, 23-26; Matt 9:35–10:1, 5a, 6-8

Scripture:
No longer will your Teacher hide himself,
   but with your own eyes you shall see your Teacher,
While from behind, a voice shall sound in your ears:
   "This is the way; walk in it,"
   when you would turn to the right or to the left.
      (Isa 30:20-21)

Reflection: It sounds too good to be true: the wheat will be rich and abundant, the lamb will graze in spacious meadows, there will be streams of running water. But best of all, your Teacher will hear and be gracious to you when you cry out, and he will walk beside you to guide you on your way.

All of this is a vision of the day of Zion's deliverance, the time of the Messiah, our time. The description of nature is idyllic and poetic, true spiritually but too good to be true literally. The part about the Teacher, on the other hand, is something we can experience almost the way it is described. Over and over again in Scripture our God describes himself as Emmanuel, God with us, and says to each of us, "I am with you; I will be with you on your way."

We find it very hard to believe that this is true. We may feel it momentarily in a moment of peace or great joy, or in the presence of beauty. But very quickly the demands and distractions and pains of the world wash in to smother our awareness of God's loving presence.

The problem is that we are dominated by our foreground instead of our background. Our foreground is what is in view, what we see and experience. Our background is our faith, our reason for living, our awareness of God's loving presence. Today our foreground has been much expanded by information technology and we are bombarded by disturbing news from around the world twenty-four hours a day. This can shake us and keep us unsettled and fearful. But if we are mindful of the background of faith that anchors us, we can handle whatever is coming at us in the foreground.

"[F]rom behind, a voice shall sound in your ears: / 'This is the way; walk in it.'"

Meditation: How much time do you spend dwelling on the betrayals and infidelities that the media offers as daily news? Do you spend as much time filling your mind from the Bible and other sources of hope?

Prayer: Dear God, we are bombarded daily by evil news from around the world. Help us to seek you in prayer and to drink from the sources of faith so that we can accept unshaken whatever the world sends our way.

SECOND WEEK OF ADVENT

December 6: Second Sunday of Advent

Landscaping

Readings: Bar 5:1-9; Phil 1:4-6, 8-11; Luke 3:1-6

Scripture:
Prepare the way of the Lord,
    make straight his paths.
Every valley shall be filled
    and every mountain and hill shall be made low.
        (Luke 3:4-5)

Reflection: Sitting at a red light, fingers drumming on the wheel, crowding out distractions lest the driver behind you has to blare out the news that the light is green now. That's one kind of waiting. A phone call: a family member deployed overseas will be home for Christmas. Ah, that sparks a very different kind of waiting. Serious house cleaning, haircuts and new shoes appearing, grocery lists multiplying on the refrigerator door, the very air alive with anticipation as the family makes everything ready for the great day.

John the Baptist knew nothing about traffic lights or Christmas company, but he did know one thing for certain: the Lord was coming. So he called his hearers to get everything ready. He puts this Advent agenda in images of landscaping. He announces the good news and sets out his preparation program in a very unpromising landscape: the desert wilderness. Empty, parched, barren, scarce on food and water, the desert speaks of utter ruin that contrasts sharply with memories of the Garden of Eden that the world once was. News photos of the Sahara turning neighboring green lands to sand or of Hiroshima on August 6, 1945, remind us that this ruin is real.

However, in John's book, the ruin is no excuse to sit back and do nothing. The journey to the heart of the desert—our hearts—is long and hard, so we'd better get to work building a road for the Lord to get here. Straighten out the road, says John. Don't make him pick his way around piles of newspapers, through life's debris, past dirty dishes overflowing the sink. Fill up those ruts, some now valleys as deep as the Grand Canyon, cut and worn hard by the tramping feet of selfish thoughts, angry words, destructive prejudices. Stamp down yesterday's molehills grown into today's Rocky Mountains because we wouldn't forgive and forget. Take the grader to the roughened washboard surfaces left by indifference and sloth to bar the way for anyone trying to get down the ranch road to the house. Then, and only then, can you stand back and watch eagerly for the salvation of God.

John has a name for this landscaping. He calls it repentance.

Meditation: Take a serious look at the landscapes of your heart. What kinds of work do you need to do to make ready the way of the Lord? What tools would help?

Prayer: Come, Lord Jesus! Give us the wisdom to see how we have blocked the road to our heart, and grant us the will to cast those roadblocks aside, strengthened by the power of the Holy Spirit.

December 7: Saint Ambrose, Bishop and
Doctor of the Church (Catholic Church)
Monday of the Second Week of Advent (Episcopal Church)

A Cure for Paralysis

Readings: Isa 35:1-10; Luke 5:17-26

Scripture:
When Jesus saw their faith, he said,
  "As for you, your sins are forgiven." (Luke 5:20)

Reflection: Three men were in a boat fishing. The day wore on without much success. One fisherman got bored and took a small drill out of his tackle box and began drilling a hole in the bottom of the boat. The other two looked around in alarm and said, "What are you doing!? You'll get us all drowned!" The man said calmly, "What I do in my part of the boat is my business."

We recognize that the driller's attitude is absurd, but sadly, we may live that way in our little world, oblivious to the presence and the needs of others around us. "Am I my brother's keeper?" (Gen 4:9). Yes, I am.

We witness a remarkable healing in the gospel story today. But it is even more remarkable than we may have noticed at first: The man on the stretcher was forgiven his sins and healed of his paralysis not because of his own faith, but because of the faith of his friends. Usually Jesus says to a healed person, "[Y]our faith has saved you. Go in peace" (Mark 5:34).

But here it is the faith of other people that draws Jesus' healing power.

We do not know if the paralytic had faith or not. He may have protested all the way. But what could he do? His friends loved him enough and had faith enough to struggle with carrying him up to the roof and lowering him, while the people inside were doubtless complaining about the interruption and perhaps the falling tiles.

The world is filled with paralyzed people who cannot help themselves. Any of us may be paralyzed at times. We do not always know how to help one another, but we can carry one another to Jesus and trust that our faith will give Jesus room to work.

Meditation: Who are the people in your life who carry you by their faith? Who looks to you to carry them to Jesus?

Prayer: Lord Jesus, we know you are waiting for us but we do not always have the courage to seek your help. Please send people of faith to help us when we need it, and strengthen our faith so that we may carry others to you.

December 8:
The Solemnity of the Immaculate Conception
of the Blessed Virgin Mary (Catholic Church)

Tuesday of the Second Week of Advent (Episcopal Church)

Getting Ready

Readings: Gen 3:9-15, 20; Eph 1:3-6, 11-12; Luke 1:26-38

Scripture:
May it be done to me according to your word. (Luke 1:37)

Reflection: Only twenty-two days till Christmas! How are
your preparations going? Today's solemnity offers us a good
opportunity to pause and think about God's Christmas
preparations and perhaps reassess our own.

Unlike many of us, God started getting things ready a very
long time ago, back at the beginning of our human story, as
we hear in today's first reading: "[Eve's] offspring . . . will
strike at your head." That was already the first promise of
the Savior to come.

Of course, God had a lot to do before that promise could
be kept: first a people of the word to form; then a mother for
the Savior to prepare, a woman born of the people of the
word, a woman so attuned to the word that she could receive
it with every fiber of her being, in her very flesh. What hinders
most of us from receiving God's word with full attention
and living it to the hilt is the original self-centeredness in-
herited from Adam and Eve. What we now call original sin
distorts our hearing and deafens us. What we cannot fully

hear, we cannot fully live. This would not do for the woman in whom God's Word, the second person of the Blessed Trinity, would take on humanity and from whom the Child would learn how to live what he was.

To fashion such a mother, God reached into the future and used the fruits of the Child's death and resurrection to free her from every hint of original sin from the first moment of her existence. The result was a woman absolutely undistorted and unhindered by any kind of self-interest. When the angel told her God's plan, a plan that surely shattered all her own, the message met with none of the roadblocks ego might have raised. Mary simply said, "Behold, I am the handmaid of the Lord. / May it be done to me according to your word." And so she became the mother of the unique Child who is both fully human and fully divine. We acknowledge the depth of that mystery when we call her "the Mother of God."

We might imagine that God could then just sit and watch all those preparations pay off. But the plan didn't stop with Israel, Mary, and Jesus. God is still busily at work in us, preparing us to say our yes at Christmas to the gift and call we will find in the manger.

Meditation: How is God preparing you personally to receive the coming Christ? What selfish perspectives and habits clutter up your ability to say yes?

Prayer: Mary, Mother of God, pray for us, that the Spirit may open our hearts to receive and to live God's word fully, according to the divine plan.

Against All Hope

Readings: Isa 40:25-31; Matt 11:28-30

Scripture:
They that hope in the LORD will renew their strength,
  they will soar as with eagles' wings;
They will run and not grow weary,
  walk and not grow faint. (Isa 40:31)

Reflection: These words of the prophet were written to encourage the dejected Jewish deportees during the dark days of the Babylonian exile. They had lost everything they had held sacred, especially their beloved promised land and the temple of Solomon. They were taunted by their neighbors that they had also lost their God, because if their God had been truly powerful and really loved them, their temple would not have been destroyed, their homes would not have been pillaged, and they would not have been exiled to Babylon.

In the civilizations of the ancient Near East, each nation or people had its own god. The local god and religion were a matter of national pride, and the subjection of another group implied that our god is more powerful than your god. If they were smart, their neighbors were saying, the Israelite exiles would admit the obvious and accept Marduk, the patron god of Babylon.

"Do you not know / or have you not heard? / The LORD is the eternal God, / creator of the ends of the earth." Against all appearances, the prophet proclaims the ancient faith and encourages the Israelites not to lose heart. He reminds them that the God they worship was never limited by territory. Their God was never the God of Israel only, but of all the earth.

As events transpired, within a few years King Cyrus of Persia would conquer Babylon and permit the Israelites to return to their homeland. But the prophet did not know that when he wrote his stirring words. He was calling on his trust in God's fidelity and was convinced that somehow God would continue to be with his people and give them the support they needed, whether or not they were released from exile.

When we ourselves are in exile, in situations when there seems no way out, the stirring words of the prophet remind us of the God we serve and rouse us to cry out to this loving and saving God in our need.

Meditation: Remember a time when you seemed to be in an impossible situation and could not hope for a solution, but somehow you came through. Thank the Lord for the deliverance that you may have by now taken for granted or forgotten.

Prayer: Dear God, often there are issues in our lives that seem to have no solution: broken relationships, financial pressures, concerns about family members. Help us to place all our problems at your feet and turn to you as our loving father.

December 10: Thursday of the Second Week of Advent

Only Words?

Readings: Isa 41:13-20; Matt 11:11-15

Scripture:
From the days of John the Baptist until now,
   the Kingdom of heaven suffers violence. (Matt 11:12)

Reflection: As grocery store music bathes us in reassuring promises of the coming of the Prince of Peace, we have to stop and ask, "What is all this about violence?"

Biblical scholars admit this is a difficult text. It doesn't refer to Jesus' own death and what his disciples would suffer. Rather, Jesus is talking about violence that began with John the Baptist and continues even as he speaks.

But this timeframe gives us at least one clue as to how to read his words. John the Baptist is still alive but has already been taken by force and subjected to violence in prison. Why? Specifically, because he spoke against King Herod's marriage to his brother's wife, Herodias. John's words provoked the king's violence. Jesus, by this time, has also provoked violence by his words. The violence is still verbal, not physical. But that too is coming. Yet John and Jesus both spoke of nothing but the kingdom of heaven.

St. Paul called God's word "the sword of the Spirit" (Eph 6:17). Jesus knew that when he said, "I have come to bring not peace but the sword" (Matt 10:34). The truth about God's kingdom was not always welcome in his lifetime and is not always welcome now. God's word of truth cuts to the marrow of our human confusions and deceptions and exposes what calls out for healing. But, perverse human beings that we are, we are not always willing to accept what the word offers, and we hurl it back violently, to the detriment of the one who spoke it.

We often underestimate the power of words, but the Bible never does. There, words always act. We sing words of peace in this season in safe places like church. Yet we often withhold words that would bring about real peace through the hard work of facing truth and seeking reconciliation. We are afraid that the reaction might be anger, rejection, a broken relationship. Yes, says Jesus, it might be, even if what we say is spoken in love. But what will happen if we stop speaking words that cut a way through deceptions, including self-deceptions, to the possibility of the reconciliation offered by God's kingdom? To be honest, we would have to stop singing hymns that promise peace, and we could not pray that it will come, this year, at the birth of the Prince of Peace.

Meditation: The tensions of Christmas preparations sometimes bring quarrels. Where does the world around you right now need words of peace? What words of peace is God entrusting to you to speak? Is anything holding you back?

Prayer: Christ, Prince of Peace, come into our hearts to make peace in us and through us by the power of your word.

Eye Problems

Readings: Isa 48:17-19; Matt 11:16-19

Scripture:
To what shall I compare this generation?
It is like children who sit in marketplaces and call to one
      another,
  "We played the flute for you, but you did not dance,
  we sang a dirge but you did not mourn." (Matt 11:17)

Reflection: The history of human fickleness goes a long way back, probably to the beginning. We see it in the story of the exodus, when Moses was charged with leading the Israelites from bondage in Egypt to freedom. At first the people were eager and grateful, but as soon as things went bad they turned against him, blaming him and even accusing him of intending their ruin. It goes so far that they forgot how desperate they were and created an imaginary bliss of their slavery: "Did we not tell you this in Egypt, when we said, 'Leave us alone that we may serve the Egyptians'?" (Exod 14:12).

The flip side of this fickleness is the blame game: I don't like the way things are, and you are the one at fault. Or, yes, what I did was wrong, but it wasn't my fault. In the Garden of Eden, the man blamed the woman and the woman blamed the snake. Social scientists speak of three determinism

theories: genetic—my ancestors are the cause of my weird-
ness; psychic—my parents emotionally scripted me to my
compulsions; environmental—it's the economy, the weather,
the boss, the spouse, the Democrats, the Republicans. We're
back to eye problems: the splinter and the plank.

It comes down to a failure to take responsibility for one's
actions, which is certainly a contemporary theme. I did flunk,
but that was because the teacher grades too hard. The car
that I was driving went off the road. Nobody reminded me
to water the plant.

Okay. I'll play the flute. You dance.

Meditation: Who or what in your environment causes you
problems? How can you make a new start with them/it?

Prayer: O God, we thank you with the psalmist "because I
am wonderfully made" (Ps 139:14). Help us to count our
blessings and accept our responsibilities so that our lives
will be an act of praise to your goodness.

December 12: Our Lady of Guadalupe (Catholic Church)

Saturday of the Second Week of Advent
(Episcopal Church)

God-with-Us

Readings: Zech 2:14-17 or Rev 11:19a; 12:1-6a, 10ab;
Luke 1:26-38 or Luke 1:39-47

Scripture:
See, I am coming to dwell among you, says the LORD.
(Zech 2:14)

Reflection: On the little hill of Tepeyac above the magnificent
Basilica of Our Lady of Guadalupe in Mexico City stands a
chapel. Small, simple, plain, bereft of the *tilma* with the astonishing image that now hangs in the grand basilica below,
the chapel still seems fragrant with the memory of the
woman clothed as if with the sun who spoke so warmly to
Juan Diego. It's somehow easier here than in the larger, newer
church to recall the young village woman who crossed other
hills to visit her aging cousin Elizabeth. She came bearing
good news, first the child in her womb and then her song,
often called the *Magnificat*. The Virgin who appeared to Juan
Diego wore the sash customarily worn by a pregnant Aztec
woman. She was again bringing her unborn Son, who *is* the
good news, to a people whose lives were mired in religious
and political violence. Robed in Aztec religious symbols, she
announced silently the advent of a new and very different

God than the ones they had known and worshiped. The God in whose name she spoke very simply, tenderly, and lovingly was the God of love whose Son was sent to be peace. This stranger from a different place spoke a very different language than the language of conquest with which the Spaniards had arrived not long before. She asked for no human sacrifice, no gold and silver, no tribute of slaves but only for a church, a place where people from near and far would gather in worship of God. Even today, the basilica is saturated with a silence that makes the faith of the pilgrims a reality one can touch, breathe, and surrender to. Under the eye of the Virgin painted on Juan Diego's *tilma*, it is hard to be less than one's best and deepest self, awed by the truth of "God-with-us"—Advent's promise still kept.

Not everyone can travel to Mexico City, but all of us can find a time and a place to step out of the pre-Christmas hub-bub into that Presence, whose silent voice still calls us beloved children, as the Lady of Guadalupe did on Tepeyac.

Meditation: Visit your parish church or find another quiet place. Shut the door on all your preoccupations. Ask Elizabeth or Juan Diego to help you to hear God's voice speaking just to you as a beloved child in ways you can recognize and understand.

Prayer: Our Lady of Guadalupe, lead us to our own Tepeyac, our inner quiet place, where we can hear God's voice speaking to us in love and respond with joy like John the Baptist.

THIRD WEEK OF ADVENT

December 13: Third Sunday of Advent

The Eyes of God

Readings: Zeph 3:14-18a; Phil 4:4-7; Luke 3:10-18

Scripture:
The LORD, your God, is in your midst,
   a mighty savior;
he will rejoice over you with gladness,
   and renew you in his love,
he will sing joyfully because of you,
   as one sings at festivals. (Zeph 3:17)

Reflection: No biblical passage expresses the warmth and fervor of God's love for his people more beautifully than this verse from the prophet Zephaniah. Picture God breaking out into song when he looks at us. What will the neighbors think!?

Zephaniah knew as well as we that God is neither male nor female. But we portray God in human terms because that is the reference we understand.

He will "renew you in his love" is a beautiful thought translated from the Greek version, but the Hebrew is even more beautiful: "He will be silent in his love." God gazes on us in silence, loving us and appreciating us, without saying anything. What is this but contemplation? God turns the tables on us. We are supposed to contemplate God, but God is contemplating us. Once a reporter asked Mother Teresa, "What do you say to God when you pray?" "I just listen." "What does God say to you?" "He just listens."

The love of God for us is here expressed in the extremes of silence and exuberant music. At one moment God is gazing at us in speechless love, at the next he is singing at the top of his voice.

If we think that the prophet's exuberant faith comes from a sheltered existence and pie with every meal, we need to read the earlier part of his prophecy that pronounces judgment on Judah and Jerusalem because of worship of false gods and unjust and abusive leaders. Even worse, "Its prophets are reckless, / treacherous people; / Its priests profane what is holy" (3:4). But this doesn't weaken his faith: "the LORD in its midst is just, / doing no wrong" (3:5).

Meditation: Reflect on Rembrandt's *The Return of the Prodigal Son* (readily available for viewing on the internet) and imagine yourself as the focus of the father behind his closed eyes.

Prayer: Loving God, we take your love so much for granted and often restrict and limit it. Help us to gaze on you in prayer so that we may show a contemplative loving face to a world toiling in weariness, hopelessness, and fear.

December 14: Saint John of the Cross,
Priest and Doctor of the Church (Catholic Church)
Monday of the Third Week of Advent (Episcopal Church)

Who Is This?

Readings: Num 24:2-7, 15-17a; Matt 21:23-27

Scripture:
By what authority are you doing these things? (Matt 21:23)

Reflection: The chief priests and elders are asking Jesus a question we've all heard: "Who do you work for?" His work has certainly invited the question. He has drawn crowds by his preaching on the ways of God and the ways to live God's word. He has performed wonder after wonder—bread multiplied, sick people healed, demons driven out, sinners forgiven, even the dead raised to life. Most recently, he has disturbed the leadership badly by entering Jerusalem in an odd triumphal procession, hailed as messianic "Son of David," but mounted on a donkey's colt. Worse, he has just chased out of the temple area the money changers and animal vendors authorized by the chief priests to exchange Roman coins for the coinage required for temple offerings and to sell approved animals for temple sacrifice. The temple coffers will suffer from Jesus' behavior. Those in charge want to know who gave him the authority for it.

What they really want to know, though, is not so much who Jesus works for as who he is. They're having trouble fitting him into their prefabricated boxes. He could, they suppose, be a prophet. Prophets were often harsh critics of temple practice, and temple leadership. Prophets did occasionally cure the sick or even raise the dead, but not usually. Prophets did speak God's word and point out right and wrong ways to live it. But they didn't claim to forgive anyone's sins. And they were humble enough to say "God says," never "[y]ou have heard . . . [b]ut I say to you" (Matt 5:21-22). There were all these hints that Jesus was more than a prophet. There were those who thought he might be the Messiah. But he didn't quite fit that box either. The messianic Son of David was supposed to be a king who would have found something better to ride into town on than a donkey's colt. He was thought to be a great warrior, like David before him, not someone who instructed the mistreated to turn the other cheek and to love their enemies. So who was this man? Should they throw themselves at his feet or arrest him? Or simply discount him as a madman to be restrained and pitied?

The question still hangs in the air we breathe. Who is this Jesus? A judge to be expected and feared, as many of the Advent readings say? A cute baby, as many Christmas scenes depict him? Something more?

Meditation: If Jesus were to turn and ask you, "Who do *you* say that I am?" what would you answer? And how does your answer affect your daily life?

Prayer: Lord Jesus, you come to us in history and mystery, and you will come again in majesty. In your great mercy, come always as our Savior.

December 15: Tuesday of the Third Week of Advent

Watch the Feet

Readings: Zeph 3:1-2, 9-13; Matt 21:28-32

Scripture:
A man had two sons.
He came to the first and said,
  "Son, go out and work in the vineyard today."
The son said in reply, "I will not,"
  but afterwards he changed his mind and went.
The man came to the other son and gave the same order.
He said in reply, "Yes, sir," but did not go. (Matt 21:28-30)

Reflection: Today's parable puts in vivid terms the saying, "My mind and my tongue deceive me, but my feet tell me the truth." We are very susceptible to self-deception, which is why we need trusted friends and mentors to help us see what we are really doing and where our life is really headed. I say I am on a diet, but my feet are always in front of the refrigerator. I say I want to help the poor, but I never seem to be where they are. Another saying, a Chinese proverb, has it, "If you keep going the way you're going, you'll wind up where you're headed."

No one is exempt from the struggle. Saint Paul has helped us by describing his own inner turmoil: "What I do, I do not understand. For I do not do what I want, but I do what I hate. . . . The willing is ready at hand, but doing the good is not. For I do not do the good I want, but I do the evil I do not want" (Rom 7:15, 18-19). Paul does not presume that he will be able to overcome this inner struggle on his own power, but throws himself on the mercy of God in Christ Jesus (7:25).

Blessed John Henry Newman realized how deceptive were his big plans, even spiritual ones, and how important it was to be guided step-by-step in our journey, as he expressed it in a hymn early in his life, "Lead, Kindly Light": "Keep thou my feet: I do not ask to see / The distant scene; one step enough for me." He returned to the theme in "Praise to the Holiest in the Height" late in his life, convinced that God had been for him "In all his words most wonderful, most sure in all his ways."

We all struggle with our motivations and are quite capable, like the young men in the parable, of fooling ourselves. We need help to be objective, beginning with prayer.

Meditation: Make a list of the top ten most important things in your life.

Prayer: Lord Jesus, we want to follow you, to be your true disciples, but our feet do not always follow the resolutions in our heads. Give us the grace to be honest with ourselves and to return to your path when we have strayed.

John's Question

Readings: Isa 45:6b-8, 18, 21b-25; Luke 7:18b-23

Scripture:
Are you the one who is to come, or should we look for
  another? (Luke 7:19)

Reflection: John the Baptist had been announcing a wrathful,
fire-breathing Messiah who would throw the brood of vipers
standing before him into the flames their evil works de-
served. And now, here is Jesus, who says of his own work,
"Go and tell John what you have seen and heard: / the blind
regain their sight, / the lame walk, / lepers are cleansed, /
the deaf hear, the dead are raised, / the poor have the good
news proclaimed to them." No fire, not even a whiff of
smoke! Could he really be the one expected? John had to ask.

It's a question worth asking as we ourselves look around
at the sorry world that stars on the evening news and makes
daily headlines on the web. We might be too polite to call
anyone a brood of vipers, but we might equally wonder
whether or when they will get what they deserve. Is Jesus
too mild to satisfy the crying need for a world made new?

What kind of a Messiah do we really long for? The answer
will depend on the place from which we're asking. If the
salvation we most want to see is an angry vengeance that
will sweep all evildoers into the flames of hell, perhaps we
aren't looking for the One who came and is to come again.

Jesus confounded expectations by appearing as a baby in a manger rather than a fully armed warrior in the tradition of King David, and he has been confounding expectations ever since. He was capable of anger, but, to draw on a pivotal phrase from The Hunger Games trilogy, he knew who the real enemy was and is. His anger is the anger of one who sees his beloved dragged into the muck by that enemy, the Evil One. He has proven that he will do whatever it takes not only to give sight to the blind, heal the lepers, preach the good news to the despairing poor but also to redeem the ones who tortured him, degraded him, and nailed him to the cross. His tactics are not fire and brimstone but unyielding crucified love because his goal is not the annihilation of sinful humanity but our transformation.

That baby we see in the manger on Christmas cards and crèche scenes is no mere figure of irrelevant sentiment. He is a statement of the extent to which God will go to come to us and gather us into communion with Christ.

Meditation: What kind of Messiah do you really seek? What kind of conversion will he require of you?

Prayer: Jesus, Messiah and Lord, make us ready to welcome and live the vision into which you call us rather than one we have invented.

Warts and All

Readings: Gen 49:2, 8-10; Matt 1:1-17

Scripture:
David became the father of Solomon,
   whose mother had been the wife of Uriah. (Matt 1:6)

Reflection: When John the Baptist was born, people who had witnessed the amazing events surrounding his birth asked one another, "What, then, will this child be?" (Luke 1:66), for the extraordinary preparation gave promise of an important mission in life.

By the same token, the genealogy of Jesus as presented by Matthew would not have held much promise for this other newborn. Ahaz and Manasseh were rulers who promoted the worship of false gods even in the temple, Rahab was a prostitute, and Tamar acted like one to achieve her goal. Behind the laconic mention that Solomon's mother "had been the wife of Uriah" lurks a sordid story of adultery and murder.

Why does Matthew go out of his way to stress these embarrassments in Jesus' family tree? We know the genealogy could be presented differently because of Luke's enumeration, which leaves out all the figures mentioned above and avoids the Bathsheba unpleasantness by substituting the prophet Nathan for Solomon (Luke 3:23-38).

In portraying the family history of Jesus "warts and all," Matthew has served us well in two ways. First, he has made it clear that Jesus shared our human condition completely and from the very beginning. He was one of us. He did not arrive with a pedigree that set him apart or put him in a special category that protected him from the consequences of sin in the world. He was truly human, one of us.

Second, the evangelist assures us that God does not insist on pedigrees in calling us to be the disciples of Jesus. We can become what God calls us to be if we are available and willing, no matter where we start. With this encouraging message urging us on, we begin today the special liturgical days of preparation for the celebration of Christ's birth.

Meditation: Reflect on your own genealogy and the twists and turns in your prehistory through which God created your unique being.

Prayer: O God, we ask your blessing on our parents and ancestors and all who have helped us in our journey of life. Help us to share with others your love that has come to us through our families.

December 18: Friday in Late Advent

A Good Listener

Readings: Jer 23:5-8; Matt 1:18-25

Scripture:
Joseph . . . was a righteous man. (Matt 1:19)

Reflection: Joseph was a righteous man because he was a good listener. A good listener is not a mindless listener. When the law Joseph had grown up obeying told him that he had the option of having his betrothed, Mary, stoned to death because she was carrying a child not his, he listened. Then he pondered. Then he chose not to make a public show of his righteousness at the cost of her shame. The law did not require him to have Mary stoned, but it did not permit him to marry her. So he came up with an alternative: he would separate from her quietly. The line between blind obedience to the law's letter and compassionate obedience to the law's Giver is a fine line to walk, but Joseph walked it.

Joseph was a good listener. A good listener is never rigid. A good listener listens with the understanding that what is heard may change the hearer rather than simply confirm the hearer's most cherished beliefs. When the angel Gabriel appeared to Joseph in a dream and told him to marry Mary after all, he gave a mind-bending explanation. The Child in Mary's womb had been conceived through the Holy Spirit. We say those words calmly enough now when we recite the creed, but they blew Joseph's previously unshakeable convictions about God out of the water, as they would for Jesus' disciples and for generations of Christians wrestling to come to terms with what they meant. At first glance, they meant at the very least that Mary was no adulteress condemned by the law but a woman chosen by God for extraordinary motherhood. Unthinkable in Joseph's experience. But he raised no objections. With his world standing on its head around him, he did as the angel asked: he married Mary and proceeded to reorganize his life's agenda around his new, astonishing family.

Joseph was a good listener. He never overwhelmed God's words with floods of his own. In fact, Joseph left us no recorded words at all. However he spoke at home and work, he had the habit of silence that permitted him to hear all his life what God said through the quiet voice of circumstance: his near-divorce, his marriage, his trip to Bethlehem; his odd sojourn in a stable among beasts of burden, stammering shepherds, singing angels, and exotic foreigners; his midnight flight into alien territory, and finally his return home to quiet little Nazareth, all because God said so. What Joseph thought about it, he never said. He simply did.

Meditation: How are your listening skills amid the season's hustle and bustle? To what words do you listen hardest, and how?

Prayer: St. Joseph, pray for us when we are deaf or stubborn, that we too might become good listeners to God's word.

Are You Really the One?

Readings: Judg 13:2-7, 24-25a; Luke 1:5-25

Scripture:
He will go before him in the spirit and power of Elijah
  to turn the hearts of fathers toward children
  and the disobedient to the understanding of the righteous,
  to prepare a people fit for the Lord. (Luke 1:17)

Reflection: The importance of John the Baptist in St. Luke's presentation of the gospel story is evident from the space he devotes to John right at the beginning of his story. Already in the womb John is the precursor of Jesus, as is shown by the series of parallels between his beginning and that of Jesus. He is also the pivot of the fulfillment of Old Testament hopes, particularly carrying forth the role of Elijah as prophesied by Malachi (3:1, 23-24).

It is sobering to remember that John, himself so important in inaugurating the ministry of Jesus, was cut off early and did not live to see the working out of the movement that he helped inaugurate. In fact, it appears that at a certain point John was disillusioned with Jesus, or at least confused by him. John had told the people that one "mightier than I" would be coming to clear the threshing floor and burn the chaff with unquenchable fire (Luke 3:16-17), wreaking harsh vengeance on sinners.

But Jesus had been healing, comforting, and preaching forgiveness to sinners. When John's disciples reported this to him in prison, he sent two of them to ask Jesus, "Are you the one who is to come, or should we look for another?" (7:18-19). Jesus shows that his ministry fulfills Isaian prophecy and makes the pointed statement, "blessed is the one who takes no offense at me" (7:22-23); in other words, blessed is one who is not turned off because of false expectations about who I should be, but accepts me as I am.

We don't know whether this relieved John's concerns. We do know that, whether in darkness or in light, he remained faithful to the end to his prophetic calling and left an example that still lights the way during the Advent season every year.

Meditation: The church is the Body of Christ, the presence of Christ in today's world. How do you respond when actions of leaders in the church or their failure to act disappoints or even scandalizes you?

Prayer: Lord Jesus, your motivation and your actions were sometimes a puzzle and a concern even to your closest associates, who might have been tempted to give up on you. Help us to remain faithful to you in your Body, the church, even when we do not see your guiding hand in what is happening.

FOURTH WEEK OF ADVENT

Unlikely

Readings: Mic 5:1-4a; Heb 10:5-10; Luke 1:39-45

Scripture:
You, Bethlehem-Ephrathah
too small to be among the clans of Judah. (Mic 5:1)

Reflection: Too small to matter, said the prophet Micah about Bethlehem. Too old to bear children, said people about Elizabeth. Too insignificant to notice, neighbors might have said of Mary of Nazareth, if they had paid her any particular attention. Once King David had come and gone, Bethlehem slipped into obscurity. Once Elizabeth became a senior citizen, still childless, she earned the barren woman's customary disgrace. Mary was simply too young and perhaps too poor to warrant any special notice. And their unborn babies? Ho-hum. Years later, the people of Nazareth would dismiss Jesus' claims to be God-sent because his mother was only Mary, his reputed father only the carpenter.

Despite gospel warnings, judgment busies itself with the constant weighing, sifting, and sorting of who matters and who doesn't. Its standards are not new. We are not the first society to recognize the rich, the powerful, the beautiful, and the useful as worthy of honor while dismissing as irrelevant whoever doesn't make the cut.

Today's account of the newly pregnant Mary's visit to her aging but pregnant cousin Elizabeth tells a different story.

The young as yet unmarried virgin and the old priest's wife both carry unborn children who will change the world. Both have been chosen for this responsibility by no less than God. I have heard it said that the Almighty chooses the unlikely to do the impossible. This encounter, unnoticed by the world at large, is a case in point.

In this regard, it is an apt preview of what is to come: the Messiah so long expected in at least some segments of Jewish society will indeed come as promised. But he will come without fanfare or parades, unless you count choirs of angels terrifying Bethlehem's shepherds—who were also held in little esteem. He will come as a mere infant, homeless except for a borrowed stable, cribless except for a rough manger, unnoticed by religious and political authorities alike until the magi draw royal attention to him. Then, except for one visit to the temple, he will disappear altogether into anonymity for thirty years.

And, long hence, his end will be as unpromising as his beginning. Until a handful of women find his tomb standing open and empty, that is. But that's a story for a different season.

Meditation: And you, how do you assess people's worth? How does your judgment affect the way you treat them?

Prayer: O God, who alone sees the depths of the human heart, free us from the burden of judging others by false standards and grant us the grace to see and treat everyone as your chosen child.

December 21: Monday in Late Advent

Stunned

Readings: Song 2:8-14 or Zeph 3:14-18a; Luke 1:39-45

Scripture:
Mary set out in those days
 and traveled to the hill country in haste
 to a town of Judah,
 where she entered the house of Zechariah
 and greeted Elizabeth. (Luke 1:39-40)

Reflection: Just before this scene of the visitation, Mary's life had been suddenly disrupted by the visit of an angel with a stunning message from God. Henry Ossawa Tanner captured the moment in his painting *The Annunciation*: a young girl sitting on a disheveled bed in a peasant house gazing quizzically at a pillar of light on the other side of the room. Suddenly, from being a neighborhood girl in a remote village she is catapulted to being the handmaid of the Lord at the center of history.

Though surprised and probably in shock, Mary does not hesitate. She sets out "in haste" to visit Elizabeth. Surely there were many things to think about in such a sudden change of direction and in planning for a journey. But there was no time to waste. The Lord has called me. Elizabeth will know how to help me, how to prepare, what I should do. And indeed, Elizabeth confirms what is happening, addressing

Mary as "the mother of my Lord." The reading from the Song of Songs captures the urgency and excitement of love: "Arise, my beloved, my dove, my beautiful one, / and come!" (Song 2:10). Even the child in the womb leaps for joy.

The church wants us to have a taste of this excitement of Mary and Elizabeth and John during these final days of Advent preparation. But the liturgy has a tall order in trying to give us a sense of expectancy when the surrounding culture has already been celebrating Christmas as a commercial holiday for weeks. We can, however, do a lot on our own, immersing ourselves in the beautiful Advent readings and prayers and customs. An additional gift for each of these final days of preparation is the "O" antiphon of the Vesper Office, which today presents Christ as a beacon of light: "O Radiant Dawn, / splendor of eternal light, sun of justice: / come and shine on those who dwell in darkness and in the shadow of death."

Meditation: What happens when a sudden shock, good or bad, interrupts your life? To whom do you turn, which way do you go, what do you do?

Prayer: Dear Mother Mary, the message of the angel broke into the calm pattern of your life and stunned you, but you responded with deep faith and hope in God. Pray for us so that we may not be overwhelmed by shocks, good or bad, in our lives but may, like you, respond with faith and hope.

December 22: Tuesday in Late Advent

The Divine Upsetter of Applecarts

Readings: 1 Sam 1:24-28; Luke 1:46-56

Scripture:
"[M]y spirit rejoices"! (Luke 1:47)

Reflection: Joy is one of the most attractive gifts of the Spirit, so it's hardly surprising that a woman saturated with the Spirit would bubble over with the youthful joy that infuses the first few verses of Mary's song, usually titled the *Magnificat*, from its opening word in Latin. God has done great things for her! All her news is good—unless you're arrogant of mind and heart, or a ruler in high places, or rich, or overfed, or all of the above.

In Mary's song, we come face-to-face with the God who turns accepted goals and priorities and judgments upside down. Whatever your applecart full of assumptions is, beware: this God is apt to upset it. Arrogance? Well, humility is more appealing, but in the self-made achievers at the top of the ladder, we often treat a touch of complacency with some leniency. They've earned it. Power? Watch any kindergarten playground to see the bolder kids already vying for some clout over the others. Wealth? The actress Tallulah Bankhead once said memorably, "I've been rich and I've been poor. And, honey, rich is better." And overfed? Watch the commercials on TV! Even if you've just eaten a good meal, they try to convince you to go get some more. And far too often, we obey, despite the alarming percentage of the world's population that goes to bed hungry.

The *Magnificat* should at least scare us a little, but that is not God's purpose in putting it on Mary's lips and ours. God is not dooming those who have chosen arrogance, power, wealth, a life of overconsumption. Mary's Child has been sent not to condemn us but to deliver us from these and all the other values and practices by which we destroy one another and ourselves.

The heart of Mary's good news is that her God and ours is not judge and jury but Redeemer. As our applecarts lie on the road with the apples rolling all over, the news may not feel good at all, but its truth is that through the One she carries, we now have the option of leaving them where they lie and following Jesus on down this road to the kingdom of God, where all that has gone wrong will be put right.

No wonder the church invites us to sing with Mary daily at Evening Prayer, "My soul proclaims the greatness of the Lord; / my spirit rejoices in God my savior"!

Meditation: In this season of gifts, for what intangible gifts are you most grateful? What blessings have caused you pain but given you freedom or made you a better person?

Prayer: Mary, Mother of God, teach us your spirit of gratitude and show us the way to freedom of heart through your Son.

Refining Our Silver

Readings: Mal 3:1-4, 23-24; Luke 1:57-66

Scripture:
He will sit refining and purifying silver,
   and he will purify the sons of Levi,
Refining them like gold or like silver
   that they may offer due sacrifice to the Lord. (Mal 3:3)

Reflection: A modern parable based on this image of the divine silversmith has made its way on the internet, "The kingdom of heaven is like a craftsman refining silver." A woman is watching a silversmith hold the metal in intense flame (1,200 degrees Celsius) to burn away impurities. He says he cannot walk away during the process but has to watch continually or the metal might be ruined. "And how do you know when the silver is fully refined?" she asks. "When I can see my face reflected in it," he replies.

This is a beautiful elaboration of the biblical imagery and apparently coherent with the science of metallurgy. It is also a very positive view of the pains and travails of life, a needed counterbalance to the idea that when we do something wrong, God runs to cut a switch. As the divine silversmith, God is doing all he can to save us from the folly of our sinfulness and help us on the path to our true destiny as children created in the divine image. Our sinful tendencies are strong, and we are not convinced by a word or two of advice. We need stronger medicine.

The challenge is often not the suffering itself but the meaninglessness of it. If we could see the point, we could accept it much more easily. But this is often the heart of the suffering, that it is pointless and getting us nowhere. We are far from being able to believe that a refiner is at work.

Nelson Mandela spent twenty-eight years in prison because of his campaign against the racial injustice of apartheid in South Africa. During the day he broke rocks or shoveled lime; at night he slept on a straw mat in a small concrete solitary confinement cell. He was forbidden to wear sunglasses in the glaring lime quarry and suffered permanent eye damage. He could have become bitter, but instead achieved inner freedom. Somehow he saw beyond the meaninglessness of the present suffering. He studied Afrikaans in order to communicate with his jailers and the government. When he was released, he was able to lead his nation to national unity and the healing of ancient wounds.

We can look on our suffering as punishment or as the refining of silver.

Meditation: Reflect on the transforming action of God in your life over the years, often through suffering, using the image of the silversmith.

Prayer: Dear God, we twist and turn under suffering and are tempted to rebel, forgetting that the divine silversmith is refining our silver. Give us the grace of patience and faith, so that we may offer our suffering as a prayer for the people of God.

December 24: Thursday in Late Advent (Christmas Eve)

Daybreak

Readings: 2 Sam 7:1-5, 8b-12, 14a, 16; Luke 1:67-79

Scripture:
[We are] free to worship him without fear . . .
In the tender compassion of our God
   the dawn from on high shall break upon us,
    to shine on those who dwell in darkness and the
      shadow of death. (Luke 1:74b, 78)

Reflection: No matter how many lights you turn on, no matter how many bulbs blink on your Christmas tree, no matter how cheerfully the fire burns in the fireplace, it will be dark tonight. For those who have no lights to turn on, no Christmas tree, and no fireplace, it will be very dark indeed. If you are reading this, you are probably not among them. Or so it seems. But in a larger sense, we are all huddled under the same tent. Saint Paul, a tent maker, warned us that the tent is wearing out for all of us. This tent of our mortality will fray and tear and leave us unprotected from death's shadow. The house lights and the Christmas lights and the crackling fire won't help then.

And most of us, however grown up, are still afraid of that particular dark night. Zechariah, father of John the Baptist, standing over his new son, born to elderly parents as the night gathered in upon them, tells us that there is no need. The shadow itself is about to fray and split and give way to a day that will break out in the middle of the night—tonight!

Tonight, we will remember once again the light of Jesus Christ, sun of justice born in a place that had no lightbulbs or Christmas trees or comforting fire, only the darkness of death's shadow lying over all the world. Except for Mary and Joseph, strangers in town, and maybe a kind neighbor or two, there was no one there to see it happen. Except for a few shepherds watching their flocks on a night shattered by angels spilling out of heaven to sing the good news, no one else had any idea it had happened. But it had: the daybreak from on high had broken through death's night sky to let in the undying light.

It's broad daylight now, this morning, but when the sun sets and the night begins to chill the spirit, remember Zechariah's promise and get ready to celebrate the promise kept!

Meditation: Zechariah's canticle promises the forgiveness of sins. Search your heart for any dark places that remain and entrust them to the Light to come.

Prayer: Sun of Justice, for whose coming we long on this verge of Christmas, shine upon all the darkness of the world and bring us peace!

SEASON OF CHRISTMAS

December 25: The Nativity of the Lord (Christmas)

The Joy of the Gospel

Readings:
VIGIL: Isa 62:1-5; Acts 13:16-17, 22-25; Matt 1:1-25 or 1:18-25
NIGHT: Isa 9:1-6; Titus 2:11-14; Luke 2:1-14
DAWN: Isa 62:11-12; Titus 3:4-7; Luke 2:15-20
DAY: Isa 52:7-10; Heb 1:1-6; John 1:1-18 or 1:1-5, 9-14

Scripture:
The angel said to them,
　"Do not be afraid;
　for behold, I proclaim to you good news of great joy
　that will be for all the people.
For today in the city of David
　a savior has been born for you who is Christ and Lord."
　　(Luke 2:10-11)

Reflection: The Bible speaks of two kinds of fear, one that is encouraged, the other discouraged. The fear of the Lord that is "the beginning of wisdom" (Prov 9:10) is better known as reverence, a pervasive awareness of God's lordship in our lives that liberates us to live in freedom and joy. The other fear is alarm in the face of danger or uneasiness caused by uncertainty, both of which can paralyze us.

The angel says to the shepherds and to us, "Do not be afraid" (in the second sense) just because something out of the ordinary has surprised you. Wait and see: this may be very good! Earlier Gabriel greeted Zechariah and Mary the same way, "Do not be afraid," before announcing astonishingly good news, and this admonition was typical in the record of biblical appearances of the Lord or a messenger of God before and after Zechariah and Mary.

Why not be afraid? Because, far from being a threat, this is an announcement of great joy. "The people who walked in darkness / have seen a great light."

It might be helpful to recall the impact of Pope Francis on the whole world two years ago. He was a messenger of joy, appearing like a bright comet in our land of gloom. His first major message was "The Joy of the Gospel," in which he encouraged us to throw off the paralysis that made some of us Christians look like "sourpusses" or "mummies in a museum," whose lives seemed to be "Lent without Easter." He said we should spread the Gospel with joy and confidence, because its victory does not depend on us but is guaranteed by God.

How do we keep this Gospel joy alive or recapture it if we have lost it? "I invite all Christians, everywhere, at this very moment, to a renewed personal encounter with Jesus Christ," said Pope Francis, "Do this unfailingly each day. . . . 'No one is excluded from the joy brought by the Lord'" (3).

Meditation: Reflect on Hebrews 2:14-15 about our liberation from the slavery of fear by the death of Christ. Does any fear hold you in captivity?

Prayer: Dear Jesus, you emptied yourself of glory to come into this suffering world for our sake. Help us to be worthy of your gift, living free from fear and bringing others into the joy of your victory.

December 26: Saint Stephen, First Martyr

The Last Chapter

Readings: Acts 6:8-10; 7:54-59; Matt 10:17-22

Scripture:
[Stephen] looked up intently to heaven
and saw the glory of God and Jesus standing at the right
hand of God . . .
As they were stoning Stephen, he called out
"Lord Jesus, receive my spirit." (Acts 7:55, 59)

Reflection: The feast of St. Stephen falls like a wet blanket on Christmas cheer. Just yesterday we celebrated the birth of the Child Jesus with joy. We gathered together, lit candles, turned on multicolored lights, sang hymns, and shared our gifts.

Then comes St. Stephen to remind us of the persecution, suffering, and death that the Child grew up to endure and promised to all his disciples—including ourselves. Filled with the Spirit, ardent of speech, strong in conviction, Stephen waded deep into debate, apparently with the force of an unstoppable roller coaster, for his opponents "could not withstand the wisdom and the spirit with which he spoke." Poor losers, they stoned him to death for blasphemy.

At this point, we get a glimpse of why we are remembering Stephen today. As he crumpled under the stones, Stephen prayed, "Lord Jesus, receive my spirit." And as he was dying, he "cried out in a loud voice, 'Lord, do not hold this sin against them,' " though today's reading doesn't get that far. And with those words, he died.

Sound familiar? It should. We're reading the story of Jesus' death over again, this time with St. Stephen replaying Jesus' words, "Father, into your hands I commend my spirit" and "Father, forgive them, they know not what they do" (Luke 23:46, 34). The word "martyr" means witness: the first martyr bears explicit witness to Jesus' own saving death.

No one could call it a pretty picture, this brutal destruction of a man armed with nothing but the Gospel. But it is a telling one. The story of Jesus' birth, which we heard only yesterday, gathers its force from the cross whose shadow falls across the manger from the future. The story of Christmas is only a sentimental tableau without its last chapter, which includes both death and resurrection. Stephen's story completes the Christmas story: his death echoes that of the Savior, even in Stephen's choice of words; his dying vision of Christ in glory proclaims powerfully that the crucified Lord is risen. To embrace Jesus in the manger, warns Stephen's tale, we must also embrace Jesus on the cross. In choosing the Child we choose the Crucified.

Stephen tests the depth of our Christmas spirit: to love Christ in the cradle, we must love Christ on the cross—not then, but now, in sufferers all around us.

Meditation: Christmas inspires many acts of charity. How will you continue to live this Christmas spirit after Christmas?

Prayer: Jesus, Savior, through the example and intercession of St. Stephen, lead us to live your story faithfully in our own.

December 27: The Holy Family of Jesus,
Mary and Joseph (Catholic Church)

Third Day in the Octave of Christmas (Episcopal Church)

One Like Us

Readings: Sir 3:2-6, 12-14 or 1 Sam 1:20-22, 24-28;
Col 3:12-21 or 3:12-17 or 1 John 3:1-2, 21-24; Luke 2:41-52

Scripture:
He went down with them and came to Nazareth,
    and was obedient to them. . . .
And Jesus advanced in wisdom and age and favor
    before God and man. (Luke 2:51-52)

Reflection: John Henry Newman once gave a powerful sermon on the Lord's Passion. After describing the suffering of the passion, Newman paused. "Then in a low, clear voice, of which the faintest vibration was audible in the farthest corner of St. Mary's, he said, 'Now I bid you recollect that he to whom these things were done was Almighty God.' It was as if an electric shock had gone through the church, as if every person present understood for the first time the meaning of what he had all his life been saying."

The same emotion might strike us while reading today's gospel, "[Jesus] went down with them and came to Nazareth, / and was obedient to them."

Christians have had difficulty from the earliest days in accepting that Jesus was completely God and completely human at every moment during his life on this earth. Believers have split off in different directions by denying the divinity (e.g., the Arians) or the humanity (Monophysites). At first it was more difficult to believe in Jesus' divinity, but later, and even up to the present, many Christians have found it more difficult to accept his full humanity, and take words like "Jesus advanced in wisdom" as only a figure of speech. Even more difficult are passages like those in Hebrews: "For we do not have a high priest who is unable to sympathize with our weaknesses, but one who has similarly been tested in every way, yet without sin" (4:15); "Son though he was, he learned obedience from what he suffered" (5:8).

When he visited Nazareth in 1964, Pope Paul VI said, "The home of Nazareth is the school where we begin to understand the life of Jesus." In Jesus' obedience in his family home, we see him living and growing up just as we did. We know that he understands our own life intimately. "So let us confidently approach the throne of grace to receive mercy and to find grace for timely help" (Heb 4:16).

Meditation: What are some of your struggles in life that you find hard to imagine in the life of Jesus? How would it help if you were able really to understand and accept that Jesus experienced completely what it is to be human?

Prayer: Lord Jesus, you seem so far above us, yet your very reason for coming into this world was to draw very close to us, becoming one of us in order to understand our struggles. Draw us close to you so that we may "confidently approach the throne of grace" (Heb 4:16).

December 28: The Holy Innocents, Martyrs

Fourth Day in the Octave of Christmas (Episcopal Church)

The Children of Bethlehem

Readings: 1 John 1:5–2:2; Matt 2:13-18

Scripture:
Herod is going to search for the child to destroy him.
 (Matt 2:13)

Reflection: In Christmas week, we read two stories about the children of Bethlehem. And what a contrast they offer: the story of Jesus' birth fills us with joy; the story of the Holy Innocents' death fills us with horror. And rightly so.

In the birth of Jesus, God speaks anew the Word of life, this time in human flesh. In the death of the Holy Innocents, the Evil One attempts to interject in its place the word of death. At issue is not the children themselves. They are murdered, but we call them "holy" to affirm our faith that they are alive now in the hands of God.

At issue is Herod himself. As grievous as the death of millions was in the holocaust of World War II, and all the other holocausts before and since, more grievous still from God's perspective is the corruption and destruction of those who dehumanized, tortured, and slew them. Jesus is God's Word of Life, but Evil works hard always to countermand it with the word of death. The Herods of history are its servants.

The birth of Jesus comes as good news. He is remembered as a child and adult with a name, a purpose, a destiny. The children of Bethlehem were bad news to Herod, for whom they concealed an anonymous threat to his power. For him, they had no name, no purpose, and no destiny except to serve as ammunition in his battle for power. In *The Screwtape Letters* by C.S. Lewis, the senior demon, "author" of the letters, says that Hell views humans precisely as cannon fodder that Evil uses to forge weapons against God, who loves as persons what Screwtape calls "the little vermin."

In a culture too often unfriendly to children, the victims of Bethlehem have become an emblem of all discarded children, cast away nameless on the streets, in crack houses, in pornographic film studios, and, a recent focus, in the disposal bins of abortion centers, because they got in the way of someone's pleasure, convenience, or ambition. They are our tragedy, but the adults who demean them, exploit them, abandon them are the Enemy's triumph in the war of evil versus good, death versus life.

The story goes on in our midst. The two accounts we read this week, the birth of Jesus and the death of the Holy Innocents, will not allow us to take it lightly.

Meditation: How do you speak the word of life in all you say and do? Are there any ways in which you speak the word of death?

Prayer: O God, keep us faithful to the word and work of life.

Fire and Cloud

Readings: 1 John 2:3-11; Luke 2:22-35

Scripture:
Lord, now let your servant go in peace;
   your word has been fulfilled:
my own eyes have seen the salvation
   which you prepared in the sight of every people,
a light to reveal you to the nations
   and the glory of your people Israel. (Luke 2:29-32)

Reflection: An especially memorable scene in the story of Jesus' nativity is the moment of Simeon's recognition of the child's identity. In the East it is the subject of icons, and in the West of paintings—by Rembrandt, Holbein, and many others.

How did Simeon know this was the "Christ of the Lord"? We are told the Holy Spirit revealed that he would not see death before this moment, and he "came in the Spirit into the temple." But how did the Spirit make it known to him?

We are leery of people who say they regularly get messages in their prayer or signs in their daily life. Most of us don't receive anything so clear, even though we might have a strong sense of being guided by God through our prayer life. We might feel calmer in the face of a problem after having spent time in prayer.

God is described in the book of Exodus as leading the people through the wilderness by means of a cloud by day and a fire by night (Exod 13:21). I think we experience this in a way, too, but not constantly—a sign from God when we least expect it, as when I prayed for days to one of the holy deceased monks for help in an important decision, and right before the meeting his memorial card fell out of a book as I pulled it off a shelf. The meeting went very well.

Sometimes the sign or message is much clearer. After Mother Teresa's death we learned that though she had experienced intimate conversations with Jesus when she was called to her work on the streets of Calcutta with his words "I thirst" for the people, once she began that mission the intimacy ceased, and she lived the rest of her life in spiritual darkness. At one point she wondered whether the earlier conversations were something she had only dreamed.

An elderly American priest stationed in Rome, who had never experienced special signs, in prayer heard a voice saying to him, "Tell Mother Teresa 'I thirst.'" This meant nothing to him, but when she received the message in a letter, it meant everything to her.

Meditation: Recall when, like a fire by night or a cloud by day, you were reminded of God's nearness: an answer to prayer, a near escape, a chance meeting, an unexpected blessing.

Prayer: Dear God, like the people led by Moses, we too walk in a wilderness, wondering which way to go. Open our eyes and ears to signs of your presence so that we may have new hope and go forward on our journey in faith.

December 30: Sixth Day in the Octave of Christmas

Steeped in God

Readings: 1 John 2:12-17; Luke 2:36-40

Scripture:
There was also a prophetess, Anna . . . (Luke 2:36)

Reflection: So strong and vivid are the classical prophets we've heard during Advent and Christmas—especially the prophet Isaiah—that we can easily forget that women numbered among the prophets of both Old and New Testaments. "There was also . . ." seems to turn the prophetess Anna into an afterthought tacked on to the more familiar figure of Simeon, whose story precedes hers in the Gospel of Luke. Simeon's song is enshrined as the Canticle of Simeon prayed nightly in the church's Liturgy of the Hours.

Anna is quieter, but no less intense. She is an aged widow who has literally lived in the temple for many years, worshiping "night and day with fasting and prayer." So saturated has she become with the presence of God in that holy place that she can recognize the Divine presence even in an infant carried in his mother's arms. And she can speak about this Child with the authority born of her years of prayer.

She speaks specifically to "all who were awaiting the redemption of Jerusalem." She has good news for these men and women who have lived a very long Advent indeed: the promise has been kept, the Child has been born and is here among us. Perhaps some of her hearers—maybe tourists dropping in to see the great temple sights, maybe pilgrims hurrying through their obligatory visit so they could get to the bazaar, maybe folks gathered just to gossip—might laugh at her. "Listen, this senile old woman thinks the Messiah has come—and in the person of a baby! Did you ever hear such nonsense?" But those whose waiting has been seasoned by the painful interplay of faith and hope that keeps us going through the dark nights of God's silences have recognized the truth when they hear it from this woman steeped in God.

Their response to the gift of Christmas is a measure of the sincere attention they have paid during their long Advent wait. Advent is just behind us too. The Christmas week liturgies proclaim aloud the good news that the long anticipated Christ has come. Anna might ask us, how are we responding?

Meditation: How have Advent and Christmas deepened your faithful listening to God's word, spoken through the season's liturgies but also through your daily life lived in God's presence by virtue of your baptism?

Prayer: Holy Anna, pray for us, that we may hear, recognize, and live the good news of Christ's coming every day.

Holy Oil

Readings: 1 John 2:18-21; John 1:1-18

Scripture:
But you have the anointing that comes from the Holy One,
and you all have knowledge.
I write to you not because you do not know the truth
but because you do, and because every lie is alien to the
truth. (1 John 2:20-21)

Reflection: In the opening words of his first major document, Pope Francis declared, "The joy of the gospel fills the hearts and lives of all who encounter Jesus." He encouraged all believers to an experience of that joy by the renewal of their personal knowledge of Jesus: "I invite all Christians, everywhere, at this very moment, to a renewed personal encounter with Jesus Christ" (The Joy of the Gospel 3).

This is the kind of knowledge that the Letter of John is talking about, not a knowledge that can be discovered by study, but one that comes as an anointing from God. Today we would call it a grace of the Holy Spirit. In the same way "truth" here is not an accurate knowledge of facts, but awareness of and communion with the ultimate reality. In the Gospel of John, Jesus identifies himself as the truth, and that meaning of truth is in the atmosphere of this passage.

The Letter to the Hebrews envisions the church as a people on pilgrimage, surrounded by a "cloud of witnesses," faithful disciples who have preceded us but are also still with us. We will be able to persevere in "running the race" only by "keeping our eyes fixed on Jesus, the leader and perfecter of faith" (Heb 12:1-2). If we keep this focus, we will be drawn ever more surely into the truth.

Beginning with Pope Paul VI in the 1970s, recent popes have called for a new evangelization, a new preaching of the Gospel. This term has various levels of meaning, but it begins with a new awareness and understanding of the Gospel on the part of each Christian, hearing the Gospel anew, opening oneself again to the truth, not mainly the doctrines of the church but to the person of Jesus. It means awakening in ourselves the anointing by the Holy Spirit that we have received as baptized and confirmed Christians. Then it may be said of us, "you have the anointing that comes from the Holy One, . . . [and you] know the truth."

Meditation: When you read the Scripture today, picture God's word as a holy oil pouring over you and anointing you with the peace that is beyond understanding (Phil 4:7).

Prayer: Dear God, our minds are filled with facts and figures, but much of what we know has no permanent worth or even present value. Anoint us with your Holy Spirit and enlighten us with the truth that leads to eternal life.

January 1:
Solemnity of Mary, the Mother of God (Catholic Church)
Holy Name of Jesus (Episcopal Church)

Mother of God

Readings: Num 6:22-27; Gal 4:4-7; Luke 2:16-21

Scripture:
When eight days were completed for his circumcision,
   he was named Jesus, the name given him by the angel
   before he was conceived in the womb. (Luke 2:21)

Reflection: Mother of God? Surely the Mother of God could do better than a manger for her baby's bassinet, and shepherds for a birth announcement? The staging is all wrong. What was the public relations department thinking?

The clue is in the Child's name, given to him formally in the customary religious rite of circumcision. In Hebrew, Jesus means "God is salvation." His birth translates into physical reality the prophetic promise of a young woman who would name her son "Emmanuel," meaning "God with us." In this Child, God is with us in our own flesh, in the midst of our own human story, which—publicity image-makers to the contrary—is rarely a story of a silk-hung birth suite, a jeweled crib, and paparazzi plastering the web with pictures of an unlucky infant who will never draw a private breath, earn a living, or know anything but suffocating splendor that removes him from all normal human realities.

Such an infant, wrapped safely away from every contact with real human life, could hardly be called "God with us" because he couldn't get near us in the world where we actually live. The Son of God becomes *our* salvation by becoming God with us where we are: God walking our streets, breathing the air we breathe, feeling the heat of the sun that sometimes burns us, eating our bread, drinking our water and wine; God speaking to us, touching us, awakening us, healing us, and forgiving us right here, right now.

And Mary was his mother. Jesus learned at his mother's knee what it meant to live among us. The evangelists respect her privacy enough not to discuss her every thought and move. But she herself has been appearing down through history as one of us—a woman of Aztec appearance at Guadalupe, a woman speaking the local *patois* at Lourdes, a woman weeping as we do at La Salette, a woman whom people in all places and all walks of life have trusted with their worries, their requests, their needs, none of them too petty for her attention.

We trust the Mother of God before we honor her because we know she knows us and watches out for us. She does so because she herself is the lovely image of our ever-present, ever-loving God revealed in depth in her Son.

Meditation: Do you talk to Mary? Do you have any relationship with her?

Prayer: Holy Mother of God, teach us to be with your Son, who is always with us.

January 2: Saints Basil the Great and Gregory Nazianzen,
Bishops and Doctors of the Church

A Precious Heritage

Readings: 1 John 2:22-28; John 1:19-28

Scripture:
Let what you heard from the beginning remain in you.
If what you heard from the beginning remains in you,
   then you will remain in the Son and in the Father.
   (1 John 2:24)

Reflection: Israeli archeologist Gabriel Barkay experienced
the thrill of a lifetime when excavating southwest of the Old
City of Jerusalem during the 1979–80 season. He discovered
two tiny silver scrolls that had been used as amulets. They
were dated to the period right before the destruction of the
Solomonic temple in 587 BC, the time of the prophet Jeremiah,
and contained the earliest occurrence of a biblical text outside
the Bible, Aaron's Blessing from Numbers 6:24-26: "The LORD
bless you and keep you! The LORD let his face shine upon
you . . . and give you peace." Barkay was able to hold in his
hand devotional emblems that had last been carried or worn
by fellow religionists 2,500 years before.

   We experience something akin to this feeling when we are
put in touch with our earliest Christian roots by texts like
the First Letter of John. After centuries of tradition, including
trinitarian debates and challenges to our faith, we are right

at home with the profession of the first-century Christians: "Anyone who denies the Son does not have the Father, / but whoever confesses the Son has the Father as well. . . . If what you heard from the beginning remains in you, / then you will remain in the Son and in the Father" (1 John 2:23, 24).

In an era of relativism and individualism, we may be given the impression that there are no eternal or unchangeable truths. Chart your own course. Form the value system that seems best for your needs. Whatever works for you.

The Letter of John takes us back to a solid foundation. "Let what you heard from the beginning remain in you." Gabriel Barkay's discovery, by the way, isn't affecting and moving only for those of the Jewish faith. It is part of our tradition, too, and Aaron's Blessing was part of the first reading yesterday for the Solemnity of Mary, Mother of God.

Meditation: How aware are you of the riches of the tradition of the church? How might you gain access to the teaching of the early witnesses?

Prayer: Dear God, in your providence you have arranged for the preservation of many spiritual treasures from our Hebrew ancestors and the earliest Christians. Please open for us an access to this treasure and give us a desire to explore the riches.

EPIPHANY AND
BAPTISM OF THE LORD

Motives

Readings: Isa 60:1-6; Eph 3:2-3a, 5-6; Matt 2:1-12

Scripture:
We saw his star at its rising
  and have come to do him homage. (Matt 2:2)

Reflection: The magi of Matthew's gospel are rather an exotic mystery. The evangelist actually tells us very little about them: they come "from the east," they have followed a star that they read as a birth announcement for a new King of the Jews, they have brought expensive gifts for the Child, and, having presented them, they disappear back into the obscurity from which they came. Readers have deduced that they were three, and three kings at that, because of the gifts. Imagination has supplied them with names—Melchior, Caspar, Balthasar. Ancient Christian writers and later hymn writers have seen them as prophets, choosing gifts that announced three essential dimensions of the Child's identity: royalty (gold for a king), divinity (frankincense offered to a God), and destined to die (myrrh for his burial).

Matthew tells us one more thing about them, perhaps the most curious thing. They went to enormous trouble and expense to find the newborn king of a fairly insignificant kingdom under Roman domination for one reason only: "to do him homage." Another common translation is "to worship him." That translation may better explain their gifts.

Before tradition assigned gold, frankincense, and myrrh specific symbolic meanings, they all played a part in the temple worship of the one God—though how foreigners from "the east" knew that is anybody's guess.

The magi came to worship the newborn Child, king of a nation not their own. They got directions at the royal palace, but they found the Child in an unremarkable house with his mother, unattended by the servants a royal child would have had. Undeterred, they fell down and did him homage, or worshiped him. They gave him their gifts without commentary. And then they left.

They asked for nothing. All that travel, all that expense, and they asked for nothing—no thank you, no hospitality, no food or drink for themselves or their servants, if they had them, or their beasts. Nothing but the privilege of offering worship to the Child.

They make me wonder, when I find myself complaining that the music at the Epiphany Mass wasn't to my taste, or the homily failed to inspire me, or the kids in the back of church were too noisy for me to pray. They make me wonder, those mysterious strangers who asked for not one single thing for themselves, not one thing except to worship the Savior I claim to love.

Meditation: When you go to church or kneel to pray at home, what are you looking for?

Prayer: Jesus Christ, born to be our Savior, purify our hearts of all the gift-seeking that keeps us from genuine gift-giving to you and to others.

January 4: Monday after Epiphany
Saint Elizabeth Ann Seton, Religious

With Eyes Open

Readings: 1 John 3:22–4:6; Matt 4:12-17, 23-25

Scripture:
When Jesus heard that John had been arrested,
   he withdrew to Galilee. (Matt 4:12)

Reflection: Taken by itself, Matthew's laconic sentence about Jesus' departure to Galilee reads like nothing more than a stage direction. But it takes on much more significance in connection with another stage direction later on. In chapter 14, Matthew will tell of John the Baptist's beheading, which ends, "His disciples came and took away the corpse and buried him; and they went and told Jesus." Then comes the second stage direction: "When Jesus heard of it, he withdrew in a boat to a deserted place by himself" (14:12-13).

We may be accustomed to think that for Jesus the path was always clear, and that he single-mindedly pursued his destiny as if following a script. But his was a human journey like ours, and though he had a sense of the direction he was to go, he had to make decisions along the way. In Jesus' reaction to the news of John's imprisonment in today's text, and later on in his reaction to John's murder, Matthew gives us a deeper sense of the human drama in Jesus' mission. But he does it like a good novelist, giving hints and leaving the rest to our imagination, which will modulate according to our own human experience.

John had announced the beginning of Jesus' ministry and implied that Jesus would be continuing the work he was doing and even taking it to a higher level: "[T]he one who is coming after me is mightier than I. I am not worthy to carry his sandals" (Matt 3:11). Now Jesus hears that John is arrested and has to think to himself: If I stay on this road, I am going to get the same treatment as John. Later on, it is even worse: If I keep doing this, I may be killed, too.

In both instances, Jesus withdraws and goes away, the second time "to a deserted place by himself" (14:13). What do you and I do when we are confronted by a shock, the sudden death of a friend or family member, the news that the company we work for has been sold? We need silence and a time alone, to regroup, to decide what we will do next.

In both cases, after Jesus withdraws for a time of reflection, he doesn't hide or cease his open ministry, but the first time begins to preach openly and call disciples, and the next time looks away from his own concerns to the needs of others, and begins to heal and feed the people.

Meditation: Go with Jesus to a deserted place after he hears of the Baptist's death and join imaginatively in the struggle going on in his mind.

Prayer: Lord Jesus, our salvation hung in the balance at several points in your ministry. You had free will and could have refused the chalice of suffering, but you said yes and suffered and died for us with your eyes wide open. Help us to be grateful and to show our gratitude by the way we live.

January 5: Tuesday after Epiphany
Saint John Neumann, Bishop

Feed My Sheep

Readings: 1 John 4:7-10; Mark 6:34-44

Scripture:
Then, taking the five loaves . . . and looking up to heaven,
  he said the blessing, broke the loaves, and gave them to
    his disciples
  to set before the people. (Mark 6:41)

Reflection: The liturgy never lets us bask for long in the warm intimacy of the little Family hidden among working beasts and known only to a handful of shepherds. The celebration of the Epiphany last Sunday began to break open the relative privacy of the stable to manifest the Savior to the wider world. In this week between Epiphany and the Baptism, we begin to get previews of the busy years of Jesus' public life.

Today's gospel serves as a bridge. Jesus was born in Bethlehem, whose name means "House of Bread." His Mother laid him in the stable animals' feeding trough, probably in a bed of the hay intended as their feed. Coincidence? The evangelists don't believe much in coincidences. They believe in the complex weave of history, where the threads of salvation appear in one place, like this stable, then disappear only to reappear in another spot, like the hillside in Galilee where Jesus ministers in today's gospel. Here we see him feeding the tired and hungry crowds first on the Word of Life, and then on mysteriously plentiful food that presages the Bread of Life. What will come much later in the story is that the true Bread of Life is not loaves broken in the field but the body of Jesus himself, broken on the cross.

But the weave of history continues to unfold. Today we remember St. John Neumann, fourth bishop of Philadelphia (1852–60). He was an immigrant who arrived in New York with one suit of clothes and one dollar in his pocket. He remained poor all his life so he could share whatever he received with others in need. As priest and bishop, he worked tirelessly to provide his people with churches and schools where they could be nourished on solid religious formation, good preaching, and the sacraments of the church.

In the manger, on the Galilean hillside, in nineteenth-century Philadelphia, and all around us today, we continue to catch glimpses of the Eucharist where Christ still feeds all human hungers on that same Word of Life and Bread of Life. Let us give thanks and prayers for those called to continue that work as St. John Neumann did.

Meditation: How have you been nourished and grown through the banquet of Word and sacrament this Advent and Christmas? How will you turn and feed others on what you have received?

Prayer: Through the intercession and example of St. John Neumann, continue, O Christ, to feed and nourish us with the Word and Bread of Life, and help us to turn and feed others in their hungers.

Finding Time

Readings: 1 John 4:11-18; Mark 6:45-52

Scripture:
And when he had taken leave of them,
   he went off to the mountain to pray. (Mark 6:46)

Reflection: "When I get some time, I will pray. I'm too busy right now." Variations of this excuse plague us all. "I've got an important project going on and I just don't have any time to pray right now."

Jesus shows us by example how to pray when you don't have time. You make time. In today's story Jesus has just finished an exhausting day teaching five thousand people until it was late, and then still later, when the disciples thought it was too late, providing food for the large crowd. They had already been tired before this, and Jesus had wanted to relax with them. "Come away by yourselves to a deserted place and rest a while" (Mark 6:31). But when he saw the crowd, his heart was moved to pity, and he took care of them. Finally, after the work was all over, he went off to the mountain to pray.

This didn't seem to rub off on the disciples. After a similar day of hard work recorded earlier in the gospel, Jesus had tried to find the solitude to pray by rising before dawn the next morning and going to "a deserted place." But the disciples "pursued him," saying, "Everyone is looking for you" (1:35-37). Jesus should feel guilty for taking time to pray when there are more important things to do.

One of the last speeches of Pope Benedict XVI before his resignation was his 2013 Ash Wednesday homily. He spoke of the rhythm of prayer and ministry: "The Christian life consists in continuously scaling the mountain to meet God and then coming back down . . . so as to serve our brothers and sisters with God's own love."

We see this rhythm in the stories about Jesus. He seeks time to be alone with his Father, but when he comes back he begins to minister to the needs of the people. In today's story he may even be interrupting his prayer to help the disciples when he sees that they are in danger from the wind and waves. He has spent time with his Father, and when he speaks to them, he sounds like his Father: "Take courage, it is I, do not be afraid!"

Meditation: What is ordinarily the best time of the day for you to go apart for a while to spend time with God? Do you find your commitment to prayer consistent or haphazard?

Prayer: Dear God, we know that our inner peace and the energy for your work come from our communion with you. Help us to stand firm against the temptations to substitute ministry for prayer or to put you off when the time of prayer comes. Fill us with your love and grace.

The Story Goes On

Readings: 1 John 4:19–5:4; Luke 4:14-22a

Scripture:
The Spirit of the Lord is upon me. (Luke 4:18)

Reflection: Once again, we see the Divine Weaver at work, as we did last Tuesday. This time the thread first appears when God takes the angel's words to Mary at Jesus' conception into the adult reality of his public life. In Mary's home in Nazareth, the angel said to her, "The Holy Spirit will come upon you . . ." and you shall conceive a son. In today's gospel, in the synagogue at Nazareth, Jesus, that Son, reads, "The Spirit of the Lord is upon me." And he says of himself, "Today this Scripture passage is fulfilled in your hearing."

Just as the Spirit of God hovered over the primal waters in Genesis 1 and carried God's Word into their depths, where it brought forth all of creation, so now the Spirit will bear Jesus' words into all the corners of human life, the dark and the light, to bring forth the new Creation—not a second humanity but fallen humanity reborn. And this creative work is no abstract idea. Jesus repeats Isaiah's promises, adding he himself will keep them in his preaching, healing, dying, and rising: the poor will hear good news, the captives will go free, the blind will see, and the oppressed will taste freedom at last.

And we are they when we are deafened to God's word by the clamor around us and within us, when we are enslaved by unbreakable habits, when we are blinded to goodness and to love, when we are burdened by too much stuff, too little time, too many anxieties. Millennia have passed since Genesis, centuries since Nazareth, but still the Word of God is alive among us, and still the promises are being kept.

Remember that Christmas is not the end of this story of humanity remade. It's a world-changing, heart-changing new beginning. So when the decorations are put away and the tree taken out, when the thank yous have all been said, when the carols vanish from the supermarkets, there is no call for the post-holiday letdown we sometimes experience. Rather, Jesus calls us to take new heart as the Spirit energizes us to take up his gift of new life, not once but every day. Even if we've already broken our New Year's resolution, Jesus has not broken his!

Meditation: As you think about returning to "ordinary time" next week, reflect on the healing and liberating renewal you have received through the Spirit this Christmas and resolve again to accept and live into these blessings.

Prayer: O Christ, Savior, open our eyes to the working of the Spirit you pour out upon us every day. Grant us the courage to accept it and share its fruits with others.

The Jesus Lift

Readings: 1 John 5:5-13; Luke 5:12-16

Scripture:
> [W]hen he saw Jesus,
> he fell prostrate, pleaded with him, and said,
> "Lord, if you wish, you can make me clean." (Luke 5:12)

Reflection: The scene in today's gospel may be the end of a long story. How many times had the leprous man sought healing, clutching at every straw that presented the slightest possibility of hope? Every time he had a glimmer of hope his life hung in the balance, because healing could change everything. As long as his condition was considered contagious he could not live a normal life in family and society but had to remain distant. Surely there was a lump in his throat every time he asked for help. He is very humble and tentative: "Lord, if you wish, you can make me clean."

Pope Francis stirred the world several times during his first months in office, but never more than when he embraced Vinicio Riva, a man suffering from neurofibromatosis, which causes him to be covered from head to toe with swellings and itchy sores. Vinicio is accustomed to being avoided or rebuffed, but the pope smothered him in an embrace. After this encounter, Vinicio later commented, "I felt I was returning home ten years younger, as if a load had been lifted. . . .

I feel stronger and happier. I feel I can move ahead because the Lord is protecting me."

It isn't only Jesus or the pope who has the opportunity to say the word or give the sign that will lift a burden for others. Philo of Alexandria, a contemporary of Jesus, is attributed with the saying, "Be kind, for everyone you meet is fighting a hard battle." Most of the leprosies or maladies that burden people are not visible, but their effects can be no less painful and paralyzing. The worst suffering is often the feeling of being alone, isolated, with no one to turn to. A smile, a helping hand, or an encouragement may do much more than we foresee. Pope Francis's embrace of Vinicio was an expression of love and acceptance, but in Vinicio's experience it meant even more: "The Lord is protecting me."

Meditation: Everyone you meet today is carrying some burden or concern you can't see. Look at each person with love and pray that his or her burden may be lifted ever so slightly.

Prayer: Dear God, you have embraced us many times when we were heavily burdened and felt unworthy of your touch. Help us not to be absorbed in our own concerns but to walk with eyes open to the burdens of others.

Best Man

Readings: 1 John 5:14-21; John 3:22-30

Scripture:
He must increase; I must decrease. (John 3:30)

Reflection: The Christmas season will end on Sunday, and Ordinary Time will begin on Monday. The passage from the quiet of the annunciation and birth of Jesus through the epiphany to the dusty roads and streets of Palestine is intensifying.

The gospels of Mark and John supply no Christmas story: no angels, no stable, no magi. Instead, John the Baptist appears in the desert—that ruined waterless land through which we so often travel—announcing that the Messiah is coming to pour out God's word like rain upon the sand, plant wheat where cactus grows, bring water for our thirst and bread for our hunger, until that Easter passage when he himself will become our sustenance.

In today's gospel, John, the voice of the announcer, says the Messiah is already at work. His followers just don't recognize him because he is not doing what they think he should. In fact, he seems even to be competing with their own teacher. They don't like it. John tells them they have it all wrong. He himself is not the star of the show. He is only the one who stands beside the Bridegroom and serves him.

That was a powerful image for hearers raised on the long love story between God and the fickle "bride," the chosen people, Israel. Today, when the best man take his place at the altar steps for the wedding, we look not at him but at the bridegroom and hold our breath waiting for the bride to appear. John is hinting at a connection no one around him could imagine between this bridegroom and the God of Israel, but he only hints. Israel has only one bridegroom, God, but that this Messiah is divine will be fully revealed much later. In the meantime, says this humble and truthful best man, it's time for me to step aside. The Bridegroom is on his way.

And the bride? Well, she will finally make her appearance only in the book of Revelation, at the end of that long love story begun in the Old Testament. The Bridegroom must first do incredible things, including die and rise from the dead, to make her ready.

We live between the first chapter of this story and the last. It's time to get dressed for the wedding. It's a long wedding, you know, from our baptism, in which we are clothed in the wedding garment, who is Christ, through the repeated feasting at the eucharistic table, to the final meeting at the heavenly wedding banquet of the Christ and the church.

Meditation: Do you sometimes get in the way of God's work? How do you need to step aside?

Prayer: Lamb of God, lead us on our way and walk with us as we travel toward God's reign brought to fullness.

January 10: The Baptism of the Lord

Giving Up Being God

Readings: Isa 42:1-4, 6-7; Acts 10:34-38; Luke 3:15-16, 21-22 or Isa 40:1-5, 9-11; Titus 2:11-14; 3:4-7

Scripture:
In truth, I see that God shows no partiality.
Rather, in every nation whoever fears him and acts
     uprightly
is acceptable to him. (Acts 10:34-35)

Reflection: There were shocked headlines a couple of years ago when Pope Francis said that Jesus died to redeem everyone, even atheists. This showed that after fifty years we haven't caught up with the teaching of Vatican Council II: "Divine providence [does not] deny the assistance necessary for salvation to those who, without any fault of theirs, have not yet arrived at an explicit knowledge of God, and who, not without grace, strive to lead a good life" (Dogmatic Constitution on the Church 16). As we see in the first reading, St. Peter said the same thing centuries before that.

Atheists have been persecuted and even murdered because of their lack of belief, but believers have also done the same to one another for differences of belief. How is it that there have been centuries of religious persecution by Christians—of pagans, of Jews, of other Christians—when we believe in a God who shows no partiality and gives everyone religious freedom?

Obviously God is much more tolerant than we are (which is good news for all of us). "People look at the outward appearance, but God looks at the heart" (see 1 Sam 16:7). Once we get something right, we're offended that others don't get it right, too. If it only goes that far it's not too serious. But when we start requiring, even by force, that people see it our way, that's when the trouble begins. For generations the waters were muddied by the axiom "Error has no rights," which was applied to mean "People in error have no rights."

One of the most significant events of the Second Vatican Council was the approval and promulgation of the Declaration on Religious Liberty on December 7, 1965. "The Vatican council declares that the human person has a right to religious freedom. Freedom of this kind means that everyone should be immune from coercion by individuals, social groups and every human power" (2). Saint Peter: That's what I tried to say a long time ago.

Meditation: Research a religion you don't understand or are even suspicious of and read about the main tenets.

Prayer: Dear God, you have created us with a desire for you, but we often take long and twisted paths to find you. Help us to be understanding and tolerant of people who take different paths from ours to seek you.

References

December 1: Tuesday of the First Week of Advent
Francis Xavier Nguyen Van Thuan, *Testimony of Hope: The Spiritual Exercises of Pope John Paul II* (Boston: Pauline Books, 2000), 42–43.

December 3: Saint Francis Xavier, Priest
Jerry Weintraub, *"Oh, God!"* (Warner Bros., 1977).

December 4: Friday of the First Week of Advent
Adrienne von Speyr, *Light and Images: Elements of Contemplation*, trans. David Schindler Jr. (San Francisco: Ignatius Press, 2004), 19.

December 16: Wednesday of the Third Week of Advent
Suzanne Collins, *Catching Fire*, The Hunger Games trilogy, bk. 2 (New York: Scholastic Press, 2009), 378.
———. *Mockingjay*, The Hunger Games trilogy, bk. 3 (New York: Scholastic Press, 2010), 372.

December 27: The Holy Family of Jesus, Mary and Joseph
James Anthony Froude, "Oxford Counter-Reformation, Letter III," in *Short Studies on Great Subjects*, vol. V (London: Longmans, 1907), 201.
Catechism of the Catholic Church, 2nd ed. (1997), 533.

December 28: The Holy Innocents, Martyrs
C.S. Lewis, *The Screwtape Letters* (New York: HarperCollins, 2009), 64, 95.

January 8: Friday after Epiphany

Ben Wedeman, "Meet the disfigured man whose embrace with Pope Francis warmed hearts," CNN (November 27, 2013), http://www.cnn.com/2013/11/26/world/europe/pope-francis-disfigured-man/.

January 10: The Baptism of the Lord

Austin Flannery, ed., *Vatican Council II: Constitutions, Decrees, Declarations; The Basic Sixteen Documents* (Collegeville, MN: Liturgical Press, 2014).